MW01041235

James 1:2-4

"Consider it pure joy, my brothers, whenever you face trials of many kinds, because you know that the testing of your faith develops perseverance. Perseverance must finish its work so that you may be mature and complete, not lacking anything."

JAZZY Kitty
Publishing & Marketing LLC.

STRAIGHT

UP

HOPE

By: Sheila Andrien

Straight Up Hope

By: Sheila Andrien

Cover design by: Andre M. Saunders

Logo design by: Andre M. Saunders

Editor: Faith Woodard

Associate Editor: Anelda L. Ballard

Photography by: Beth Glick and Photobucket.com

© 2008 Sheila Andrien

ISBN# 978-0-9768540-7-4

ISBN# 0-97688540-7-4

All rights reserved. This book is protected under the copyright laws of the United States of America. This book may not be copied or reprinted for commercial gain or profit. The use of short quotations or occasional page copying for personal or group study is permitted and encouraged. Permission will be granted upon request.

Scripture quotations are from the New International Version, King James Version and Recovery quotations are from the NA Basic Text Fifth Edition.

For Worldwide Distribution

Printed in the United States of America

Published by Jazzy Kitty Greetings Marketing & Publishing, LLC

Utilizing Microsoft Publishing Software

ACKNOWLEDGMENTS

I would like to thank the Lord Jesus Christ who died so that my salvation was possible. To God be the Glory for His amazing love and amazing grace. Without the love of Jesus, which was shown to me-not preached to me, my life would have never changed.

I would like to thank my lovely daughters Amanda and Jessica, also my father for loving and encouraging me to carry on and follow the narrow path.

Thank you to the congregation of The Ark Bible Chapel for loving me, showing me a better way and faithfully praying.

Special thanks to Beth Glick for putting up with me as we put the photos together.

Thank you to Anelda Ballard, my publisher. She came up beside me and told me it was possible.

Thank you again Jessica for the cover shoot.

Thank you to the hair stylist, Amanda Hart, who provided a haircut and the makeup for the photography.

Special thanks to Tim Whiteside for prompting me to compile the poetry and consider publication.

Thank you to everyone who inspired a poem. Finally, Glory once again; be to God for blessing me with the gift of poetry.

DEDICATIONS

This book is dedicated to Skip Eagle, Anna Brey, Ida Glick, the congregation of The Ark Bible Chapel in the town called Woodchoppertown, PA. Yes, Woodchoppertown is a real place.

Read this to know my story and find hope. Hope for everyone who desires. **YES... EVERYONE!!!**

Jesus didn't come for the well. He came for the broken, the lost, the sick, the hurting and the people the world has forgotten. **He came for you and me.**

TABLE OF CONTENTS

TABLE OF CONTENTS

TABLE OF CONTENTS

INTRODUCTION

This is a book of wonderful grace and peace through Jesus when the cards seem stacked against you. When people seem mean and you have given up on being happy, that would be the time to read this book. We all get discouraged and the points I want to make in this book are that crabby and miserable are choices. You have to decide if you want to experience life or just exist. Deuteronomy is an excellent example of this After 40 years of wandering and grumbling Moses asked his people do you want to enter the Promised Land or do you want to stay in the wilderness? He said "I am a dying man I am imploring you to look to God and get it right." This would be what I am trying to achieve through this book. I want you to know that I understand grumbling, complaining and hopelessness. I also understand freedom in Christ and want to offer it to you.

Deuteronomy 30:15-20 NIV *15 See, I set before you today life and prosperity, death and destruction. 16 For I command you today to love the LORD your God, to walk in obedience to Him, and to keep His commands, decrees and laws; then you will live and increase, and the LORD your God will bless you in the land you are entering to possess. 17 But if your heart turns away and you are not obedient, and if you are drawn away to bow down to other gods and worship them, 18 I declare to you this day that you will certainly be destroyed. You will not live long in the land you are crossing the Jordan to enter and possess. 19 This day I call the heavens and the earth as witnesses against you that I have set before you life and death, blessings and curses. Now choose life, so that you and your children may live 20 and that you may love the LORD your God, listen to His voice, and hold fast to Him. For the LORD is your life, and he will give you many years in the land he swore to give to your fathers, Abraham, Isaac and Jacob.*

INTRODUCTION

Deuteronomy 19 states that God cried out for His children to get it and look to Him. I think He still hurts and grieves when we go astray. We know the deal, we know what the right thing to do is and we still manage to find the wilderness. Actually, if you are anything like me, you will notice it is not a very long walk from the Promised Land to the wilderness. Depending on my circumstance, I can get there real quick. I don't enjoy seeing anyone stuck in the wilderness. I feel so powerless. It's even harder to accept when it is you in the wilderness. While this is a story of struggles and adversity, do not be discouraged and take heart. This book has a joyous ending. You will read a marvelous message of being hopeful in any circumstance and also of finding the resources to change or endure difficult circumstances.

The following *Serenity Prayer* is a prayer used in 12 step groups:

God grant me the serenity to accept the things I cannot change;
Courage to change the things I can; and wisdom to know the difference.
Living one day at a time; Enjoying one moment at a time;
Accepting hardships as the pathway to peace;
Taking, as He did, this sinful world as it is, not as I would have it;
Trusting that He will make all things right if I surrender to His will;
That I may be reasonably happy in this life and supremely happy with Him
Forever in the next.
Amen. Reinhold Niebuhr /1943.

GROWING UP FAST

Growing up in a home with two parents, two children, and a dog; I still never felt like we were in a "Leave it to Beaver" episode. I was compared to my sister quite often and really never felt like I fit in. There was nothing wrong with being compared to my sister but we were two totally different individuals. She got straight A's, was a cheerleader and was quite popular. She was one year ahead of me in school and when I would meet my teachers they always said, "Oh, you are her sister." I found that really difficult and I think I went out of my way to prove I was nothing like her. I was Sheila and wanted to be remembered as such, not "her" sister.

I was mentally confused at a very young age. My first suicide attempt occurred when I was around seven. I laid books on top of my pillow thinking I would smother myself. Needless to say it didn't work. I frequently punched my face and fell down staircases trying to get attention. I have no idea why I felt this way. I am diagnosed with bipolar disorder and often wonder if this was the disorder manifesting at a very early age. At age twelve I discovered cigarettes and marijuana. At age thirteen, I was having sex. At age fifteen I was pregnant and the stress that came with that caused me to miscarry. Life was truly insane. If there was a rule, I went out of my way to break it. I had no boundaries and I feel like my parents were too busy arguing amongst themselves to set many limits. You also need to realize that this was 1978 or so, and people just weren't talking about addiction. Addiction was that nasty thing that happened in the inner cities to poor black children, not white middle class kids in suburbia. They were in total denial and didn't know what to do.

At age sixteen, I was married and my sister went to college. With us all out of the house my parents proceeded to get a divorce. I guess they really did stay together just for the kids. This was truly a divorce for the record books. My parents were burning pictures, tires were getting slashed, and houses were getting cleaned out as my grandparents claimed the house was a wedding gift only to my mother. My father got screwed out of equity of a home he lived in and fixed up for over twenty years. **NICE...** I already had a strained relationship with my parents because I felt they allowed me to leave because they didn't know how to deal with me. This ugly divorce really didn't help me want to make amends with them. Every child wants their parents to work things out and I truly believed with my sister and me out of the house, they would work things out. My heart sort of broke when I realized that the reconciliation was never going to happen.

My mother and I never had a good relationship. Holidays were always stressful. She never had time to spend with me but would spend money on holidays and birthdays on stuff that I never needed.

Often these gifts would be delivered after the holiday had passed. If you don't know someone on a personal level it is hard to buy a gift for them. She would always talk about how much she missed me and how happy she was to see me. I always felt if you live one hour away and you miss someone, you should visit. I always felt she came around out of obligation or guilt. Therefore, the poem Holidays with Mom states, we probably should've lied and said, "The holidays were great!" We should have just avoided seeing each other all together.

When my mother died, we finally made peace. Unfortunately, it was two days before she died. I am grateful we found peace but I wish we could've put the stuff aside and enjoyed each other at an earlier date. For those of you playing along and taking notes at home there is a lesson in there. If you can't see the lesson just pick up the phone and say, "Hi Mom," before it is too late. I'm sure you will figure it out.

I probably would not or could not write this poem today. When you first get clean, your emotions are quite raw. I had a lot of anger and was still blaming others for my stuff.

MOM

I don't understand how you can be so cold?
I'm getting older, I'm growing old,
And still I long for your soft caress.
A mother's love they say is best.

But I wouldn't know,
The pain inside, you've hurt me so.
I try to be strong, say I don't care,
But look at my heart,
You'll see the tear.

Scars inside you'll never know.
Betrayed again, I'm hurt I'm lost.
You'll never know a love like the one you tossed.

A MOTHER'S LOVE

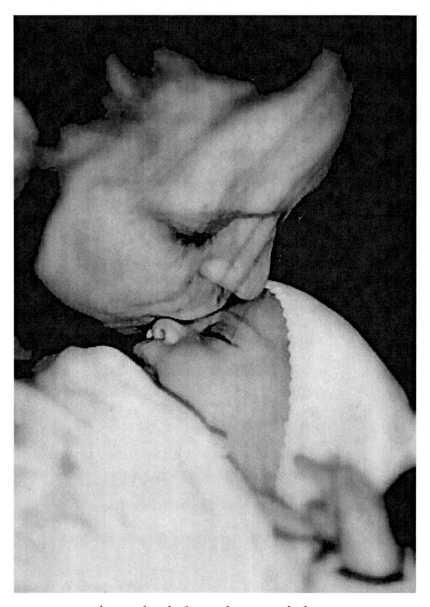

A mother's love they say is best.

HOLIDAYS WITH MOM

Holidays coming, here we go,

You make me feel bad don't you know.

Yes, it's me I'm still alone.

I didn't spend much, money is tight.

Say something you mean.

Let's not fight.

Your third husband makes me scream!

Can't take much more, seems like a bad dream.

Couldn't I leave and just go home?

I'll tell everyone you love me,

And you can call once in a while.

Hey don't sweat it, I'll put the card in my file.

Listen, I just need to tell you who I was so that you can relate. Please don't get discouraged; the best is yet to come, as well as more examples of the dysfunction surrounding family life.

There were always awkward moments; I would stick up for me cousin when no one else would. After dinner I always seem to be on dish patrol. As the family gathered for holidays it was difficult to stay more than two hours because know one knew what to say. We might have faired better talking about the weather. As deaths in the family occurred I felt the focus was on money and possessions. I did not feel the love and support or the empathy that I felt my family should give.

I never felt like I belonged. I never fit in. I hated myself and thought I was not the person anyone had wanted me to be.

Self Portrait of a Lady in Pain

This was given to me in the mid 1980's by a friend who felt my pain and understood where I was. This still pretty much applies except I am not as attractive. I am older and heavier and you pretty much have to look inside to see me now. At five years clean I still have self esteem issues.

She would like to claw away at her face, she told us, so that people would stop seeing things in it that had nothing to do with what she was like inside. She was ready to die at anytime. She said, "Because what men and boys thought about her and tried to do to her make her so ashamed, one of the first things she was going to do when she got to Heaven, she said, was to ask someone what was written on her face and why it had been put there."

Update

Today, I still wonder what people see when they look at me and I still care what they think. There is still a part of me that wants to fade away and just hide in the multitude of everyday people. The problem with everyday people is that they are just content. I want more. I want to shine like a diamond in the rough. If God has the power to transform (which I know He does) I want to make sure you know about it also. How can we be content with everyday when we can be extraordinary everyday people? God gives so much more than we can imagine. I'm not going all rosy on you. It is a struggle and it is a ride, but it is so much better than it ever was. There is a certain peace in knowing **Philippians 4:13 NIV** *"I can do all things through Christ who strengthens me."* I know that I have real friends today and I will weather the storm and not pack up-no matter what.

LIFE IN THE FAST LANE, NO HOPE REQUIRED

This was written at age 16 or 17. I was married and still going to school. I was feeling quite a bit of freedom at the time. If I got in trouble at school, they called my husband who just laughed at them. I was partying while other kids had a curfew and couldn't come home stoned. My home was the place to get stoned and there certainly was not a curfew. By the way, this particular poem was an English assignment submitted to a county contest and somehow it won second prize. It is called Me.

ME

A lot has happened since the day I was born,

I found a world of hate and a lot of scorn.

Found a lot of people with crazy hopes,

A lot of loonies who couldn't quite cope.

So many people have gone insane,

People who died their struggle in vain.

I'm right there; I'm next in line,

I'm fighting along with the rest of the blind.

Looking for dreams that never come true.

Working away with goals to pursue.

I never really realized what happened to me,

But now I think I'm beginning to see.

I'm tired of the form, I'm ready to change.

I'm moving over to the very next lane.

No one to tell me what to do,

Free to be me, how about you?

My first marriage lasted twelve and a half (12 ½) years, and was very abusive. We dealt drugs, stole anything not nailed down and were unfaithful to each other. It was not a physically abusive marriage but it was abusive in every other sense of the word. After a day of excessive drinking and speed, I tried to shoot myself in the head, but I couldn't do it and shot my leg. It was only a 22 gun and the bullet went right through my leg. In pain and not sure what to do, I drove to the hospital. This introduced me to my first psychiatric ward at the age of nineteen. Not discouraged by the incident, we continued to shoot speed, do acid, drink too much and smoke weed. We also indulged in entirely too much sex. I frequently drove across state lines with drugs and my daughter in the car and really didn't care about too much. At one point, police, trying to arrest us, surrounded our home and we had to flush all our drugs down the toilet. This was a little too close for comfort and it prompted us to move to the country.

It was at this time, I had my second child. I was having trouble walking while pregnant because I had previously broken my leg in a motorcycle accident. The doctors decided to remove the plates and screws in my leg after the baby was born. Since our home was a commune anyway, we offered a young girl a place to stay. She became our babysitter, as I was on crutches and could not carry my daughter.. She became the one my husband would leave me for. I told him I thought we were changing our lives, he told me where to go and that was that.

He saw the girls for two years until I found out his new wife (our previous babysitter) was abusing my youngest daughter. Nothing sexual but she would spank her and let her cry in the crib for long periods of time. My daughter had beautiful curls in her hair and one day when I went to pick her up, all her hair was cut off. I went to the county children's services to report my ex-husband and his wife. Children's services made up a treatment plan, which was not followed, and he has not seen his children since. It has been about fifteen years and he has a grandson and two sweet girls that he doesn't know. This is his loss and I am so blessed by those children, it is amazing. I love them with all my heart and I am so grateful that I changed to the point where I appreciate and cherish them.

F
R
I
E
N
D
S

It occurs to me that people serve a purpose in our lives and then they sort of fade away. If you have a few good friends that are there consistently, you are fortunate. We move on as if pages and chapters within a book. Such is our life. We turn the page or start a new chapter. This is the circle of life. Friends can also be compared to ingredients in a homemade soup. We add and dilute until the flavor is fabulous and we want seconds even though we are full.

THOUGHT WE WOULD BE FRIENDS

(Thought We Would Be Friends was written when I was hard-core into my addiction and still married to my first husband.)

You ripped my heart and watched it bleed,
Now you're not there to fill that need.

All the things I thought we had,
Tossed to the side and now I'm sad.

Love, trust, honesty, hope,
Thrown away for a bag of dope!

Always thought we would be Friends,
I have to let go it's got to end.

The line *always thought we would be friends*, is really poignant. I truly did believe we would always be Sunshine and Hitman; those were the nicknames we acquired on the streets. He has not called or visited his children in fifteen years. If he saw his children at the mall he would not recognize them.

Glancing at life these fifteen years later, now this poem almost seems more appropriate for someone in my life today. I guess time does heal most wounds. There are always people you think you will grow old with. Unfortunately, life shows up and you don't know where they live by the time you are 40, 60 or 90 years old, and so it goes. People are like chapters in a book, we just turn the page.

We met a family and shared every aspect of our lives with them. The friends' home was one where you could just walk in. Their kids would stay over and I would send mine. We spent holidays with them and took vacations with them and they even shared our dog at times because they didn't want one all the time.

For all the lies we told and crimes we covered up, there was one lie I couldn't keep. The husband of this other family became sexually involved with a thirteen (13)-year-old girl. He met her through his daughters and said "He was trying to help her because she was suicidal and depressed." He said "He fell in love with this girl." He sent his family to the mall so he could be alone with her. He confessed to me he had sex with her. She was the same age as our kids. I told him to knock it off before the police came around, but he didn't. He begged me to lie for him; he said, "Age didn't matter because in other countries it would be acceptable." I couldn't do it. I went to court and told the truth. When subpoenaed to court, I told the truth and lost my friends. That was a most difficult decision to make.

They offered him six months in jail and counseling if he would admit he was wrong. He wouldn't. He received a mandatory minimum of five years state time. A good fifteen (15) years later, he is still in Gratersford State Prison.

His wife divorced him and she hung up on me one time when I tried to call. The kids I considered my own have never spoken to me since. He never wrote. I think when I wrote this I felt that everyone eventually leaves you and moves on with their lives. Thus FRI ends. (Which stands for friendships end.)

FRI ENDS

A word, just a word we use casually.

With imbedded meanings,

You can see if you look with open eyes.

Like a tiny seed we watch it grow,

Like a child we help it develop.

This bond that links me to you,

Careful it's a crystal chain.

Crushed with the lightest touch,

The most beautiful things in life are delicate or easily lost.

If time pushes me aside or

Heaven forbid we break the chain.

Baby remember my name.

FRI ends, even if only for a day!!!

The Sunshine Kid

This was written for me by the man who is now in prison. What we think and what life becomes is sometimes very different.

ALWAYS WELCOME

How could I stay angry?

How could I not forgive?

A raging fire,

You burn within me.

A sudden rain you comfort me.

Your pain, your joy, your confusion lives within me,

Are parts of me?

Of all the worlds this pilgrim has visited

None ache with beauty,

Blaze with sorrow,

Or dance with delight

As does yours.

In it

I felt

Always Welcome

Always Needed

As you are.

He Remains Anonymous 9/1/87 for S. Hart

THE FOLKS

The people I considered close,

The ones I thought were friends,

Have left me standing all-alone

And it's raining once again.

Praise you in the storm,

You say I'm growing now.

But I feel lost and hurt,

And oh, I just feel down.

Carry on I've got you.

Somewhere I know it's true.

Every once and then again,

It's hard to see it through.

I can say the words and feel it.

Its seems so real just then,

But when I'm going through it,

I don't know where to begin.

(Continued)

THE FOLKS

Lord lift me up so I can sing,

So I may smile for you,

And feel your grace around me,

And your promise may come true.

FADED FRIENDS

Friends are gems in the bracelet of life.

FADED FRIENDS

I haven't seen Anelda in quite a while.

I haven't seen Marilyn in quite a while.

I hope her kids are well.

I got great news yesterday and I need someone to tell.

The other day I saw Sue, her husband passed away.

There I was in the pharmacy,

Wondering what I should say.

How do we get so caught up in life that friends just fade away?

Watching someone grieving not knowing what to say?

People I should call, people I should see,

Sometimes wishing they would all leave me be.

Friends are gems in the bracelet of life.

Why do we let them fade or hear that they passed away?

Why don't we cherish the special people that touch us?

Why not make memories for another day?

CRASH AND BURN-
WHERE IS THIS ELUSIVE HOPE?

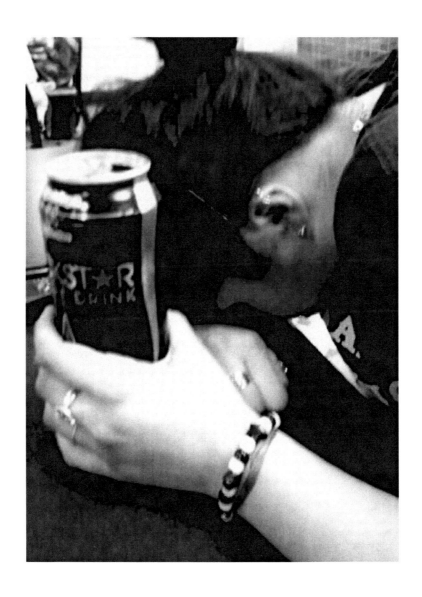

The party swings into high gear after the divorce as I was sexually **Active** and frequently woke up with people whose names I couldn't remember. I got to the point where I would make porn movies or prostitute myself to get high. My relationships were incredibly abusive at this time, sexually and physically. It makes me sick to think of them. I thought that I was no good and deserved this type of treatment. I was held hostage one time in my own home by a crazed boyfriend. This is just a sampling of the insanity that twenty-five plus years of addiction have cost me.

I was arrested several times. I was bitten by my pet bobcat and acquired cat scratch fever. No, I am not going to explain that. It is just another example of how crazy my life was. The strange part, again, is that the unacceptable was acceptable and it never occurred to me to change. I just thought it was what it was. My parents weren't speaking to me and going home was never an option.

Suicide is a very permanent solution to a temporary problem.

My actions caused me to become suicidal and I wound up in more psych hospitals than I can count. I tried many different ways to kill myself but God had a plan. The first try was a gunshot through my leg which caused no permanent damage. I overdosed on pills many times, only to be living and breathing hours later and cursing God. However, for whatever reason, He chose not to give up on me. I hung myself, only to have the ceiling collapse. That is amusing now but not at the time. I cut my wrist darn near off; you should see that scar. This was right after my first husband left me and I had no oil in the tank and had to cancel all the credit cards because they were in both of our names.

I can't even remember the various ways I tried to kill myself. I became quite insane and there were periods of time when I would hide under the bed or in a closet and just sit there crying. Not only would I hide from the world but I would do this for hours.

Speaking of suicide, my mother's second husband and I were very close, as we partied together. After the divorce with my mother, he moved close to my daughters and me. I would visit him often. When his girlfriend left him he couldn't handle life and he killed himself with a gunshot in the forehead. I walked in to his home and found him in the bedroom. I was so hysterical I spent a month and a half in a psych ward on Ativan. Now there's a drug! As a result of being in the hospital, I lost executor ship to his estate. He had willed everything to me and my girls but after it was all said and done, I received nothing, because I was not mentally capable to fight for my rights.

The moral of the story is that suicide is a very permanent solution to a temporary problem. If you kill yourself and have everything written out, there is no guarantee it will work out the way you planned because you are dead and people are unpredictable.

LESSONS LEARNED

Now, let's turn around a little bit and look at where God was in all this.

1. My first marriage was not a marriage and I am much better off without him.

2. I learned that guns are dangerous and I don't want one anywhere near me.

3. God has a plan; if He doesn't want you to die you won't no matter how hard you try.

4. Suicide is selfish and the ones you leave behind suffer most. There is always a way out.   (Continued)

LESSONS LEARNED

5. As a result of other people's greed I learned that the greatest treasures I will ever know will not be found in a bank statement, home or luxury car but will be within my heart.

6. I know today that I have treasures I never thought I wanted and I currently would not trade them for anything. I also do not have the treasures I always sought and I no longer desire them.

7. YES, I am rich in ways many people cannot understand.

At this point in the story I am probably 30–32 years of age, as I got clean and saved at age thirty-six (36). Just a little more chaos and then we'll get to the happy part. The insanity continued and I hadn't learned a thing. So how do you stay clean?

At some point, around October 1998, I had been attending AA (Alcohol Anonymous), was trying to stay clean and managed to obtain eighteen months clean. I met Brian, Skip Jeff, Bobby and Tracy. We developed a support group of all newcomers and Skip, who had nine years clean, and who knew Brian from the old days. The problem with this was we rarely attended meetings and we were swapping sex partners faster than socks. The only thing that was different was we didn't use. When Skip died of a brain aneurism in November 1998, we were all devastated.

The support group, ragged as we were, all wound up using. It really wasn't much of a support group we had formed. We had no foundation. We had no recovery. As of today, I have eight and half years clean, Brian is drinking and I have no idea where everyone else is.

During Christmas 1998, after Skip's demise and my relapse, I was downright depressed about the whole holiday thing. Brian and I decided to get high. Around 3 o'clock am I decided to call it a night but he wanted to continue. We got in a rather awful fight and my daughters woke up. They were screaming and I didn't want them to see this so I told them to go to bed and I would take Brian home. We continued to physically fight in the car and at one point he was choking me with a baseball bat as I was trying to drive. We were near his house at this point and he didn't want to go home. He continued to choke me and I stabbed him in the shoulder. (Even tough guys scream like girls when stabbed). I ran out of the car towards his mother's house where he was staying. I told her what was going on and by the time I told her the scoop, Brian was in the house and the police were outside because the neighbors had heard us. The police arrested me because I refused to say he hit me and when they tried to handcuff him I said, "What are you arresting him for? I stabbed him." SMOOOTH move! I was incredibly co-dependant at this time. I was trying to protect the one I loved. I wound up in county jail, but my daughters paid my bail the next day. Charges were dropped in May 1999, but that is another part of *"The Story."*

GLIMMERS OF HOPE

After being released from the county jail, I kind of decided to get and stay clean. I attended an AA meeting and asked a woman there what she was doing afterwards. She said she was going to a bible study. I said, "Oh." She gave me directions and told me if I got home and changed my mind to call. I paced the 16 X 20 ft. living room in my empty home.

People in recovery say people, places, and things will take you out. This is a recovery saying that basically means change your friends, change where you hang out and get rid of the paraphernalia. Given that bit of information I couldn't think of anything to do or anyone to call. Therefore, I called this woman and got directions to the bible study.

At this point I had two black eyes from the fight that left me in jail, had lost a good portion of my hair, and had bruises throughout a large percentage of my body. Trust me when I say it was a knockdown drag out encounter fueled by lots of cocaine. Relax, it gets better.

I walked into the bible study and met an old woman who offered me homemade pie and tea while everyone else was reading and discussing the bible. They were looking at the Book of Daniel, which I have since realized that people have varied interpretations of this very deep book of the Old Testament.

This woman noticed I didn't have a bible or a clue. She talked to me and asked me what was wrong. When I explained the situation, she did not appear to be shocked or appalled. She simply stated that if I prayed and looked to Jesus it would be okay. I kind of cringed at the whole Jesus thing but I had to admit she was listening and had homemade pie. I hadn't had homemade pie in probably over ten years.

As time went by I felt a little better and felt I could go home and not use. For anyone going through detox on the street, you know that it is not an easy task.

Here's the cool part, she asked me to read the sinner's prayer before I left and ask Jesus into my heart. I liked her and felt it was the least I could do, since she offered me pie and was understanding.

I read it, got saved without knowing it and have since found a relationship with my Lord and Savior, Jesus Christ. This woman's name is Ida and she is truly tight with God. When she dies, I feel she will go up to Heaven like Elijah or Jesus. I believe Jesus will personally escort her to Heaven. She is a true inspiration to our community.

Please take time to read my poem titled Poem for Ida. If you have not accepted Jesus, please recite the sinner's prayer, and ask Him into your heart. He accepts you as you are and there are no requirements, other than willingness and openness. Repentance (asking forgiveness for stuff) is helpful. It is only helpful if you truly mean it. Okay, sermon ended.

GAME ON!

IDA

She is kind and gentle, sincere, loving, and meek.

POEM FOR IDA

(Ida, if you are reading this, I love you and owe you a lot.)

I walked up to the porch and knocked upon the door,
I could never have imagined the gift that was in store.

She welcomed me with a smile and said,
"Won't you please come in and sit down."
Then she took another look and said,
"Dear child, why is it you wear that frown?"

I told her of my troubles, that I had no hope in sight.
And then she told me something that changed my life that night.

She told me I was forgiven if only I'd believe,
In a man that she called Jesus, whose love I could receive.

I thought yeah lady that is just great,
You're one of those Jesus freaks!

But she was kind and gentle, sincere, loving, and meek.

She told me that I had a chance to turn my life around.
If I'd ask Jesus in my heart and take what she had found.

(Continued)

- - - *30* - - -

POEM FOR IDA

I sat and knew she loved me although we had just met,

It was a real and caring love, like none that I'd known yet.

At that point I was truly lost; I knew that she was right.

I figured I would try this, if hope could be in sight.

She handed me a little card that contained a little prayer.

She told me just to read it aloud and hope would soon be there.

I felt the weight be lifted as I asked Him in my heart.

And though I had a troubled path I made a fresh new start,

And truly as I stand here, you would not believe,

The difference that the prayer has made,

The love I have received.

I found a brand new freedom, a different path to take.

You never know what you might find when

A new friend you make.

A SINNERS PRAYER

Lord Jesus,
Right now I invite you into my heart.

JESUS,
I believe you are the Son of God

JESUS,
I confess that I have sinned and ask for forgiveness, and I receive you into my heart.

Dear JESUS,
Thank you for forgiveness.
And I believe the blood of Jesus has cleansed me from my sin.

Lord Jesus,
Give me the Holy Spirit.
And I will follow you to the best of my ability.
I am born again and a legal child of God.

Dear Jesus, you are my Lord.

Signed _____

Date_____

You may print and laminate this or do as you wish. Just hang on to it and watch the blessings. This is also a good rededication tool. In Christ's love

Sheila.

Okay, now that we are all saved and tight with Jesus, let's pick up where we left off.

I stayed sort of clean and was still hanging with Brian at this time. I had a relationship with Dan and Anna who became angels in my life. Dan was the local handyman and he took an interest in me as he heard from Ida that I got saved. Ida went to church with Dan and Anna.

They counseled Brian and me, as we struggled to figure out the God thing and stay clean. I must tell you that the Ark (Ida and Dan's church) is a Mennonite church and they had no experience with drug addicts. I honestly believe they were learning from us as we were from them. We became the poster children for drug and alcohol addiction at the church. These people truly showed us the love of Jesus. They had bible studies with us, provided childcare, and became our friends.

There were also neighbors that I knew were Christians who would put groceries at my front door. They will never admit that, but God and I know the real deal. From December to May 1999, Brian and I occasionally used. This caused the church to wonder how this could happen. They couldn't understand why you would want to use if you knew it would cause you pain. Anyone who is an addict or knows an addict knows exactly how this could happen.

Anyway, on May 5, 1999, I was at Anna's and told her I felt like using. She prayed over me and told me to go home and ask Jesus to take the obsession away. I already had the dope in my pocket. Needless to say, I went home and stuck the needle in my arm.

Now when you stick a needle in your arm you are taking a big risk, as you don't know what is in the baggie. It could be poison, spiked or incredibly potent. It is really a toss of the dice.

Side note: Isn't it amazing how we will trust a dealer in the street but not the people around us who care for us.

Anyway this particular bag was cut with something. I started to get sick and thirty (30) minutes later I was throwing up, losing control of my bowels, and my lips were turning blue. Brian put me in the shower and assured me it would be all right. I wasn't so sure. He said if we called an ambulance the police would be at our door.

Scared I was going to die; I yelled out of the locked bathroom door to my daughter and asked her to call an ambulance. They arrived and transported me to the local hospital, which is twenty (20) minutes away. On the way there, the attendant stated that we were six minutes away and she didn't think I would make it. The other attendant said, "She's just a junkie, we were just waiting for this to happen. I just feel sorry for the children but what can you do?" I'll tell you what I did! I was so angry with that woman I fought to live. If I could've moved I would've smacked her. Remember, I just got saved, hadn't stayed clean and was not very spiritual. I would've cursed too but I was puking.

I fell into a coma for a couple weeks. Brian left and my daughters found themselves alone the next day. They called Dan and Anna who took them in. Dan prayed over me and sat with me everyday until I woke up. Once awake, the doctors said I needed my gall bladder removed. I said, "Go for it!", as I didn't realize it was to your benefit to have one. Who knew? This is the organ that allows you to have hot wings!!!

Anyway, when I got out of the hospital children's services said I could no longer have the children in my home anymore. Anna was upset with me for lying to her the night I used. She didn't understand addicts and didn't realize that if they are speaking it is probably a lie. She said she would watch the children but really didn't want to be my friend. I asked her why she prayed for me before when I was in the hospital but didn't want to talk to me now.

She said, and I quote, "I just didn't want you to go to HELL!!!" Needless to say, even though they were watching my children we weren't really talking. Now when you take responsibility away from a drug addict it just gives them an excuse to use more. Also at this time, my job said they wanted me to stay out of work and get things together. I spent the summer avoiding my children, going to counseling, cheating on drug tests, and staying high for days on end while trying not to get arrested too much. Brian was upset with me and wound up in jail early June of that year as the result of a DUI. (Driving Under the Influence.)

As September came around my counselor, who was court ordered, knew I was goofing around. She said either I get help or she would see to it I lost custody of my girls for quite some time.

I called my insurance and they would not fund inpatient treatment for me. She worked some magic and got me a scholarship to a well respected facility. I have stayed clean ever since.

REHAB
IS
FOR
QUITTERS

R.I.F.Q.

My mother wanted nothing to do with me at this point. I called her and asked her to watch my kids while in the rehab and she refused. My father wasn't capable and I had no clean friends. I felt very alone. I wasn't even sure I wanted to get clean.

My mother and I forgave each other and found peace a few days before she passed away a good six years after I was in rehab.

The state wanted custody of my children. Thank God for Dan and Anna, my new friends from the church. They rescued me from that heartache and continued to watch my children. I had no choice, I had to be there.

Dan and Anna disciplined the youngest by spanking her (a practice I never believed in) and I freaked out. I had the girls removed from their house. My Ex-mother in-law watched them for about five days and then called and said that she couldn't watch them anymore. I left the rehab early because no one would watch my children. Consequently I couldn't get a ride home from rehab and had to get staff to drive me even though it was against their policy. They couldn't release me to the streets. Everyone was done with me. They had enough.

The only thing that sustained me in that rehab was letters from Ida. She sent me a letter of encouragement or a small picture to put in my room every day. When I got out I asked her why she did such a thing and she said "It wasn't her, it was Jesus in her."

And given that bit of information I said to myself, "HUH?"

Please…come to the rehab with me. (Remember, not spiritual and barely clean.)

I also need to tell you that my clean date is September 11, 1999. How's that for a cry for help? (9/11 better known as 911)

This is when you sit in the cafeteria watching everyone visit with his or her family knowing darn well that no one is coming for you.

VISITATION

Visitation 1-5,
Don't know how I will survive.

I feel so empty, all alone,
Your family is here; it's the Twilight zone.
I watch you laugh and then you hug,
I want to mess you up or smoke a drug.

I envy you most of all.
The love you receive doesn't seem small.
The smaller things are big you see,
And family is important to me.
I miss my kids, I want them here.
A hug from them would make my year.

I know the time is coming soon,
When I'll sing a different tune.
I'll come home; we'll fuss and fight,
But most of all I'll hold them tight.
And they'll say, "Mom I'm glad you're home."
I'll have the greatest love a woman has known.

KIDS

The following poem, Kids, is pretty self-explanatory. I believed it could be better at home. I also believed somehow it was going to happen through God.

I was also very angry at the idea of someone else raising my girls. I must also say that while I had poetry to vent with, I was still feeling quite stuck in that place and was looking for an escape route. The second day of rehab I walked away from the place only to be about a ¼ mile away from the place in the pouring rain with a carton of Marlboro and a bible in my backpack. It was pouring down rain. I was soaked and couldn't really figure out where I was supposed to go as I had two children, a job and a house. The situation wasn't bad enough to go on the run for. I walked back up to the rehab, did some explaining and was dried off in time for supper.

KIDS

You need your mom?

You bet you do!

I'm so confused, what should I do?

I want to run and yet I stay,

All I can do is PRAY, PRAY and PRAY!

I asked the Lord to watch over you,

To keep you safe and see you through.

I know God's grace has brought me here.

In His arms He holds me dear.

Now it's time to learn and grow,

Relearn all I think I know.

I need change in all my life.

To teach me love, patience, and how to be kind.

Jesus loves me this I know, for the Bible tells me so.

The following was also written in the rehab.

4EVERLOST

I feel alone, it feels so strange.

Lost again, hopes out of range.

I want to laugh, I want to cry.

I don't fit in and I don't know why?

Friendship's gone!

Trust is broken!

I need to just let go and find a friend.

Can I speak, could we chat?

But my story is mine and that is that!

You smile at me and I just sigh,

You try to be nice, but I just cry.

I need to find that place inside,

Where love is love and I am fine.

4everlost was my E-mail address for years.
It is currently living4jesus@***************.
Yeah baby, it's all good now.

My oldest daughter Amanda didn't speak to me for quite a while after I left rehab. She moved out of the house the moment she graduated from high school.

Today we talk a lot. I have a grandson and love to watch him. I help her when I can and I feel our relationship is solid. What a difference a day makes. One day at a time.

We actually made homemade applesauce together the other day and we share a special kind of love, an unconditional love. It's the kind of love a mother and a daughter have. My youngest daughter Jessica and I have that bond also. However, between Amanda and I it wasn't always so. I value my girls so much today. Amanda (my oldest daughter), you mean the world to me.

A DAY AT A TIME

What has gone wrong?
You drifted further away from me.

What has gone wrong?
Addiction, guys, teens, and fights,
How do we rebuild?

Love and hope and inner strength,
A day at a Time, change and progress and lots of love
One day at a time.

My apologies to Amanda. This appears to be a rather sappy poem. It was written in rehab as the counselors asked us to reflect on family. OH MY!!! Again, they were asking me to write about a child I barely knew. I had been so self-centered. I had just left her to grow up pretty well on her own. I reemphasize that now we can talk and laugh. Jessica was small and adorable and even though she felt the damage, somehow I feel she came through a little better.

AMANDA

You were daddy's fishing buddy,
A long, long, time ago.

I've watched you struggle.
I've watched you fall,
And yes I've seen you grow.

A bright young lady you've become,
Though the attitude makes me numb.

A shining star hidden within,
Open your heart and let love in.

Be the girl I know you can be,
With an open mind your soul is free.

The following poems were written for people that were in rehab with me. Chuck was also on a scholarship and Sierra's parents wanted her to go to rehab. Rumor has it that it currently this year 2008, it costs twenty-eight thousand dollars (28,000) for a thirty (30) day stay at this institution and they will not accept insurance. It has to be privately paid. They are one of the highest rated facilities in the United States… and I doubt you can get a scholarship from the street today. Sierra was nineteen (19) and I was thirty-six (36). Chuck was probably between the ages of 30-35. I saw Chuck on the streets one time. He said he relapsed. I never saw him again. I called Sierra when we would've had one year and her parents said, "She's not here," and slammed the phone down. I called back and gave them my number. She never called back.

Chuck was a lot like me. We were hiding behind the mask we needed to wear. Given any situation, any setting, we created the ability to blend, to seem a little less whacked. There is good in all of us but after we have been judged so many times we just don't feel like showing it.

CHUCK

Black, vile, dark as night.

What you portray is quite a sight.

Death, destruction, and mayhem…PLEASE,

When I look inside that's not what I see.

Caring, warm, and quick with a smile,

He'll open the door, go that extra mile.

You make me laugh, you watch me cry.

When all alone there's a tear in your eye.

You hide the pain with the picture you paint.

A scary sight, you make the weak faint.

But tear down the walls and you will see,

A scared loving man, he's a lot like me.

SIERRA

You are like my very own,

I want the best for you.

The warmth that connects us like a fire,

Our friendship truly grew.

I've walked the road, I know the pain.

I want you not to ache, not to stumble, not to fall.

The gifts of the program are there to take.

Peace, serenity, happiness, love,

I want these things for you.

That you may grow and

Get to know a power greater than you.

You're an amazing, sweet, bright young girl.

But there's always room for change.

Grab the program and 12 steps,

Even if at first it seems strange.

Watch the flower deep within

Blossom to a rose.

And all the highs to which you'll rise,

Are mysteries God only KNOWS!

SORRY

How do I say I'm sorry?

This was written as I came home from rehab and realized that most people had not forgiven much of anything. Some were down right angry. I later learned that I had to work on myself before anyone would forgive me. Who knew?

SORRY

The pain so deep inside me

It cuts me to the bone.

Of all the things I've said or done,

The people I have known.

How do I say I'm sorry,

For the wreckage of my past?

How do I start to make amends,

And make forgiveness last?

Part of working the 12 steps of NA is writing them. The third step is simply: We made a decision to turn our life and will over to the care of God as we understood him seeking only his will for us and the power to carry it out (NA Basic Text.)

This is my "third step" before I knew what it meant.

Dec 11, 2003 or 2004

ONLY GOD KNOWS

Do you believe in the power of love?

I want to hold you my precious dove.

To feel your heart beat next to mine,

Everything will be just fine,

If you trust in God divine.

Though all around me is darkness,

And earthly joys have flown.

My Savior whispers His promise,

Never to leave me alone.

Lord I am learning there is a lot that I can't do.

I can't control my life the way that I want to.

I can't make people be what I want.

I can't stop the pain inside of me.

I can't even fully submit to your plan yet.

(Continued)

ONLY GOD KNOWS

But I know I can do one thing now.

I can make a decision to turn my life over to you.

Making the decision doesn't mean I have to make it happen.

It doesn't mean I understand your plan.

It doesn't mean I'm entirely willing.

But it means I know your will is right.

Lord, turn this decision into a reality.

Watch the flower deep within me blossom to a rose.

And all the highs to which I'll rise,

Are mysteries of life, which only God knows.

THIS

IS

MY

LIFESONG

This section is a collection of poetry and short narrations written at various points in my life. These are emotions and situations you just don't see coming. These very real times in life can blindside you. Times such as a loved one's death, Christmas, work, and Thanksgiving are examples of this. I am convinced you can relate to one or two of these.

DEATH IS A REALITY OF LIFE

Death is a reality of life. Sometimes we see it coming, sometimes we don't. Anyway it comes, it still hurts.

DEATH

The Lord called home a friend today.

I didn't see it coming, it came so fast.

Heavenly peace that lasts.

We should rejoice because he knew the Lord

Instead I cry because he left a void.

Some people touch us so deep,

The hurt seems more than we can bear.

We know that Jesus called him home, he's in Heavenly care.

But there's a hole and we miss him, and

We want to see him smile.

Still knowing we should be rejoicing, and

Praising all the while.

Bittersweet symphony, confusion in my mind

Do I rejoice? Do I cry?

I'm glad he's with Jesus; while sorry he's not here.

It's just so hard to lose the ones we hold so dear.

My friend, God speed to you. Tell Jesus I said "Hi'.

And could you please ask Him to carry us

through the following days,

The days that we truly miss you.

And let us look to Jesus to guide us in our ways.

Lord, I miss Ned

Someone asked me the other day what I wanted from life. I said I just wanted to be happy. He asked if I was in a fantasy land and was looking for Disneyworld. I said no. I just want to be able to walk down the road, pick flowers and smile. That is all I ask. He said if I would not carry all the burdens around with me I would have more room in my hands for the flowers. Simply, if you are anxious about things and go for a walk, you will have your head down and continue to over-think things. It's like looking down and picking up stones. Soon the stones will weigh you down and you will go home tired. If you kick the stones and look for the flowers it will be a more enjoyable walk.

FLOWERS AND STONES

Pick the Flowers, Kick the Stones

It's hard to do when trouble is knocking at the door.

PICK THE FLOWERS, KICK THE STONES

Where is the focus?

What is on your mind?

Flowers, stones they are not the same.

Surviving life is a treacherous game.

Attitude of gratitude, positive thinking, and more.

Pick the Flowers, Kick the Stones.

It's hard to do when trouble is knocking at the door.

Faith or fret, flowers, stones?

A new day dawning or same old stuff.

The choice is yours.

And you have to ask,

What emotions are behind my mask?

Is your head held high?

Are your wings spread?

Are you preparing to look up and fly?

Pick the flowers, kick the stones.

The decision my love is yours alone.

Give it to God, put a smile on your face.

Walk with Him covered by His grace.

Problems, blessings, what do you have?

Sunny days, cloudy skies, flowers, or stones?

Written Thanksgiving 2008:

GIVE THANKS

The scars of life, they say, are etched upon one's face.

All the scars I have acquired are covered by His grace.

All the battles I have fought I've not fought on my own.

The battle belongs not to me,

But to the one who's on the throne.

Give Thanks

I have seen the rainbow after the rain.

I've experienced His glory after the pain.

I've watched flowers blooming: the beauty of it all

I've sat and watched the snow gently fall.

Give Thanks

I have seen God's grace extended to the broken man.

His path made clear when he didn't have a plan.

Amazing grace, Marvelous grace.

Give Thanks

When a loved one dies and you cry out,

When there is little faith and a lot of doubt,

Look beyond yourself, remember salvation and Give Thanks.

(Continued)

GIVE THANKS

Through it all we laugh and cry.

We often question pleading WHY GOD WHY?

We look for answers within our mind.

And if we'd give it to God the answer we'd find.

Give Thanks

And through it all He's patient,

And through it all He's kind.

His love knows no boundaries.

He'll help us fly.

Give Thanks

In a quiet moment, we humbly bow

And we give thanks.

Life is a journey not a destination.

Struggle, struggle, and struggle with letting go of a loved one recovery and still I know that some people just don't get it and die in the streets. For this reason I am very scared.

FALLEN STAR

The waves crash down,

I'm in the middle of the storm,

And I'm trying to stay dry.

Sometimes I'm so, so lost I wish that I could fly.

Far, Far, Far away to a different place and time,

Leave my troubles far behind and walk in all Sunshine.

I look through the clouds and still see black.

Often I wonder if there's any turning back.

A sacred vow that's what I took,

Often I want to take another look.

Peace be with you wherever you are,

Often I think of you as a Fallen Star.

Along the way it wasn't always peaches and cream. I seem to write most fluently when hurting.

ROUGH

The narrow path.

ROUGH

I said "It's a rough spot."

He said "Just be strong."

I said "But I'm struggling."

He said, "Just hold on!"

Don't know if I can do it.

He said "Reach out your hand."

But I'm falling.

Fear not, I'll carry you through.

Trust in me with all your heart.

I said "Sometimes that is the hardest part."

I felt so scared, so afraid,

I dropped to my knees, together we prayed.

Sometimes you have to just let go.

It's hard to know which way to go.

The narrow path is the one to take,

The name of Jesus you mustn't forsake.

When all you can do is hang on,

Because if you let go...you just might drown!

HIDING

Peeking out just to observe.

Not quite sure when I wrote Hiding but it appears that this is appropriate at most points in your life. There are always times when life just seems cruel and you just want to take your ball and go home. Spirituality could fix that but we don't always see that in the midst of the storm.

HIDING

In a tiny corner of my world,
In a tiny spot where I can hide,
Safe and warm I hide within.

Peeking out just to observe,
Don't belong I just look on.
Are they secure or happy?
Can they sleep well at night?

Peace, love, goodwill toward man.
Do they understand?

Forgive, forget, love thy brother,
Concepts new to them.
I'll stay in, won't play today.
But, I'm content with me.
I've treated folks fair.
Let my conscience be free.

JESSICA

Quiet, Calm, Full of Love.

Just to know her it is quite obvious,

This child is truly a gift from above.

JESSICA

Quiet, calm, full of love,

Just to know her it is quite obvious,

This child is truly a gift from above.

We been thru it, that's for sure,

But through it all she finds true joy.

You'll find her reading a book, as it is her favorite toy.

Bring you a milkshake just because.

A pillow fight in the middle of the night,

Just trying to make you smile and show you it's alright.

Some things you just don't see coming and

Jessica was one of those things.

I felt scared and trapped, alone with a baby,

But I fought for custody and said, "Well maybe?"

I struggled along; it must have been tough,

But she never quit and said, "I've had enough!"

(Continued)

JESSICA

Clean and serene for eight years now,

Life is better and Jessica is my sunlight through the rain.

At 17 she plays like a child and knows how to cook.

Radiant beauty, she causes young men to take a second look.

And yet she is humble,

A Child of God,

Compassionate,

And quick with a hug.

Her light shines and I often feel she doesn't recognize it but,

No one said it is easy being 17.

This is a humorous look at sleeping in a queen size bed only to find our big old hound dog lying beside me.

BLUE

I don't know how to say this,

Except it's getting bad.

Really can't explain my life,

Some folks say it's sad.

You see,. I woke up the other morning,

Didn't know what to do.

I was really rather embarrassed,

You see my arm was wrapped around Blue.

Even though I was quite tired, and I was in quite a fog.

There's something I think you should know,

BLUE is my faithful DOG.

I know I miss my love and I don't like to be alone.

But I'm not really ready, to trade him in,

For that smelly dog with the bone.

ISAIAH 43:18-21

Streams in the wasteland.

God can do amazing things. If you don't know the lyrics to Amazing Grace, find them and read them.

ISAIAH 43:18-21 NIV

Forget the former things

Do not dwell on the past,

See, I'm doing a new thing

Now it springs up, do you not perceive it?

I'm making a way in the desert,

And streams in the wasteland.

The wild animals honor me.

The jackals and the owls,

Because I provide water in the desert

And streams in the wasteland.

To give drink to my people, my chosen

The people I formed for myself

That they may proclaim my praise.

This was written for a boss I had who didn't seem to know what is important in life, but I'm sure you can't relate to that. Just turn the page... like chapters in a book, as people disappoint, we just turn the page.

NUMB

Do you play?

Are you for real?

Can you conceive what it is to feel?

Never have I seen you smile,

While you crush my spirit all the while.

I try so hard!

Do you not know?

Your criticism is a deafening blow.

I feel sad for you and I don't know why.

God gave you wings but you can't fly.

I find freedom, I can fly,

I have a spirit and I can cry.

Even in my darkest hour grace finds me,

God's my tower, I want to feel joy.

I love to laugh,

I know that I'M ALIVE!

This was written after my best friend when I found out he had HIV. The sad part is he didn't believe this and wrote Bull at the bottom of the page. Ironically I haven't lost him to HIV but he is currently in county prison on drug charges. Did I mention addiction is cunning, baffling and powerful? This was written May 2001. It is now September 2008 and he continues to struggle with addiction.

AIDS

The pain so deep inside of me,
Thought I could cry no more.
I didn't know what was happening.
I swore God slammed the door.

There I was so happy, free, and full of life,
Then reality hit me, cut me like a knife.

Didn't know what to do.
Couldn't bear losing you.
And yet I knew God was there,
And Jesus loves me too.

Trust the Lord with all your heart.
That's what they say to do!
(Continued)

AIDS

But when it comes to this one,

I just don't have a clue,

And yet I know that when you hold me,

Everything's all right.

Take my hand and say a prayer.

We'll make it through the night.

Know that I am with you,

I'm right here by your side.

God said "He'd watch over us."

And I don't think He lied.

It's not fair, don't compare.

This is a way to relate emotional distress to physical pain. When you go to a doctor's office or emergency room they always say "On a scale of 1 to 10 what is your pain level?" I think certain things in our lives cause greater anxiety. These are our sevens. One week at church I was asking for prayer for something that was causing me great distress. My best friend was on the streets using drugs and I think I was praying for him to stop and find his way home. In my opinion this was a five at least. Someone else (lets say Carol) was in the chapel crying because worship had not gone as well as she would have liked this particular morning. I said to one of the other women in the church, (let's say Roxanne), that I didn't understand why Carol was crying. I mean geez, just chalk it up as a bad week and hopefully next week will be better. Roxanne told me to notice that Carol was crying harder than I was. She explained, what feels like a seven to me, might be overwhelming to Carol. God gives us what we can handle. Fives are fives and sevens are sevens, no matter what is causing the hurt. Carol's pain was as great if not greater than mine, no matter what caused it. I never looked at it that way before. Things that I can brush off can cause others great pain and things that cause me great pain others can tolerate. We are individuals and we have individual hurts. You can't look at what is causing the pain and you must look at the individual, console, sympathize or empathize. Look at the situation and ask yourself, "What should I do to help that person get through this today?" Therefore, I say to you, God knows what He is doing and above all else, remember it's not fair don't compare.

PEOPLE WHO JUDGE DON'T MATTER…
PEOPLE WHO MATTER DON'T JUDGE

She has cancer but my leg hurts.
She has a nice house and I've just lost my job.

What is a seven, what is a five?
Where's the gratitude for being alive?

Reach out to others in God's love,
Seems I've heard that command from above.
God carries you through no matter your lot,
You can't look at what you have and have not.

You can't judge another's pain and grief,
Or look directly in their heart.
You just need to encourage them and show them where to start.
And sometimes all they need, is for you to listen.
No solutions required.

SILENCE HAS A SOUND

Do you know silence has a sound?

If you listen hard it's very profound.

Again, trying to save my friend. Knowing darn well the only one I can save is myself.

SILENCE HAS A SOUND

Do you know that silence has a sound?
If you listen hard it's very profound.

Only a whisper in your ear,
Gently saying, do not fear.

Last night I had a bad dream,
I woke up feeling kind of mean.

It was about drugs and fights and stuff,
Oh, Dear Lord I've had enough!

Then I heard the gentle voice.
I love you it's your choice.

So it's up to you to listen too,
For the gentle voice that speaks to you.

LIFE CRASHED

Sometime life seems shattered.

Jesus is the answer, the calm within the storm.

In any given situation you have a choice. Is it, "I can do all things through Christ who strengthens me," or is it, "I can't and this is hopeless." Do you ever say, "Let go and Let God?" The other question is did you notice this is the second poem mentioning crashing? Sometime life seems shattered.

LIFE CRASHED

Did you know today my world came crashing down?
Crashing down around me and it didn't make a sound.

I looked up to Jesus because I didn't know where to go,
He said, "Girl you'd be alright if you would just let go."

I hold on to many things, things I can't control.
Then my life becomes a mess and I don't know where to go.
Jesus is the answer, the calm within the storm.
My tower in my weakness, my rock without a form.

I don't know where I'll find Him, He's everywhere it seems;
The homeless and the helpless, the righteous and the free.
I just pray that Jesus is the light that shines through me.

Let go, let God.

This is a saying I have heard at many twelve (12) step groups and also in several churches. It basically means that you should not carry all those burdens around with you. We were singing at church one day. I was overwhelmed and crying, when a woman put her arm around me and led me up to this big wooden cross. We knelt and she asked me to leave all my problems at the foot of that cross. She told me Jesus would take care of the rest. It was a very freeing experience that I will never forget. The lyrics we were singing were, "Where the wrongs we have done, and the wrongs done to us, were laid there with Him, there at the cross."

So, are we capable of doing that or do we take it all back? How easy is it to let go and let God? Do we always feel the need to put our will back in the mix? If it was so easy, I guess it would not be a slogan we need to hear over and over.

DRIVING WITH GOD AND ASKING HIM TO PULL OVER FOR DIRECTIONS

So we're driving down the road of life,

A road I've never saw before, a road I just don't know.

I look over and ask Him, "Which way are we going to go?"

He looks over and smiles, then says, "Sit back enjoy the ride."

I look over and ask, "Guess you would be my guide?"

We go a little farther and I begin to fret.

Just like a little child, I say, "Are we there yet?"

He must have found it amusing for He just smiled again.

I said, "Well, how much further, do you know the way?

There is a valley up ahead I think that we are lost.

Let's pull in for coffee and see what a map would cost?"

He said, "My child, it's not yours to know,

Just enjoy the ride."

Put your faith in Me dear child,

We'll reach the other side."

EVOLVING CHRISTMAS POEMS

This was written before I knew Jesus. Notice the spelling of Christmas. In my addiction, my family would go out to eat on Christmas and tell me straight up, I was not invited. I guess they were justified. However, on this particular year, I was just grateful I was invited to the meal. Also, I always found Christmas to be over commercialized and I was trying to steer my family out of materialism. Finally, I thought peace was something I would like to try. Feel free to compare the Christmas poems.

XMAS

Xmas is a time of joy,

Laughing kids and a brand new toy.

But let's give thanks that we are all here,

The ones we love and hold so dear.

Let's remember that XMAS is love,

Peace on Earth a gift from above.

Let's give thanks we have something to eat,

A place to come home to and shoes on our feet.

Let's try to keep that feeling alive for the rest of the year.

This was written when my friend found out he had HIV, he relapsed and wounded up in jail. My faith was quite strong at that point and I wanted to tell everyone they could change and it would be better. Alter call at the Ark 2001.

THE GIFT

It's Christmastime and here we go.

It seems we're not happy unless it's a box with a bow.

But I received a gift of a more lasting kind,

A special gift available to all of mankind.

I found peace and a brand new me,

Best of all, this gift was free.

I asked Jesus into my heart,

And in exchange I got a brand new start.

My sins were forgiven, whiter than snow.

That gave me a comfort like I've never known.

Because He died there on the cross,

My debt was cancelled He paid the cost.

I don't have to use to just to get high,

The Holy Spirit allows me to fly.

(Continued)

THE GIFT

And I know peace like I've never known.

In the midst of the storm He waits on the throne.

And if I give all my troubles to Him,

He'll carry me through and the battle we win.

He's always there, He never let us go.

He's as faithful as the seeds I sow.

If I reach out He's always there,

If I let go I get quite a scare.

You see I've been given forgiveness through His great grace,

Wonderful Mercy, sin with no trace.

I've been given salvation, the promise of what's to be.

And through Jesus Christ I've been truly set free.

I want to tell you this gift is available to all,

The big, the strong, the weak, the small.

The righteous, the filthy, the whores in the street.

If we just take the time and Jesus we meet.

I ask you now to give it a try. Accept this free gift

And together we'll fly.

This was written on the second Christmas that I was saved. There is excitement even though life isn't great. My parents never came to any Christmas service at the Ark, even though I was so excited about this new-found gift. It was difficult and disappointing but Jesus carried me through.

CHRISTMAS

Jesus was born in a manger,

So He could live

And He could teach.

So He could die

So I could live.

I know I'm forgiven I know You paid the bail.

I'm sorry you had to do it with a cruel harsh nail.

I don't feel like I deserve it,

And yet you thought of me.

Paid the price for all our sins, so us sinners could be set free.

My family is quite broke, this month has been rather hard.

I've been trying to find Jesus and I haven't sent a card.

And we don't have many presents,

You see money's been kind of tight.

(Continued)

CHRISTMAS

But we have the greatest gift,

We have Jesus to fight our fight!

There's a certain kind of calm, a certain kind of peace,

Knowing that He died to give my life a new lease.

Sometimes I really stumble and I've been known to fall,

But I really don't have to worry because I know

God has got it all!

I feel I'm at a crossroad,

Not sure which way to go.

But if I set my sites on Jesus, I'm sure He'll let me know.

I know I'm not alone here.

We all have demons to fight.

Please take a little comfort knowing Jesus was born that night.

NOW, LET'S TALK ADDICTION

If you are starting in recovery get a sponsor, a home group, and a support group. Things happen but we can't use. No excuses, no matter what!!! Because not many of us enjoy the consequences that come from using, we are looking for the great escape. I need to repeat, do not use, **NO MATTER WHAT.** Staying clean needs to be a priority. **Fear not, THERE IS ALWAYS HOPE.**

All from NA Basic Text:

We lived to use and used to live. Very simply, an addict is a man or woman whose life is controlled by drugs. We are people in the grip of a continuing and progressive illness whose ends are always the same: jails, institutions, and death. (Who is an Addict? Page 3)

We know that we are powerless over a disease, which is incurable, progressive and fatal. If not arrested, it gets worse until we die. We cannot deal with the obsession and compulsion. The only alternative is to stop using and start learning how to live. When we are willing to follow this course and take advantage of the help available to us, a whole new life opens up. In this way, we do recover. (We do Recover Pages 88-89)

Now we know that the time has come when that tired old lie, "Once an addict, always an addict," will no longer be tolerated by either society or the addict himself. We do recover.

"And acceptance is the answer to all my problems today. When I am disturbed, it is because I find some person, place, thing or situation--some fact of my life--unacceptable to me, and I can find no serenity until I accept that person, place, thing or situation as being exactly the way it is supposed to be at this moment."

LIFE HAPPENS

It's all fun and games until someone gets hurt.

It's all fun and games until someone gets shot.

It's all fun and games until someone goes to jail.

It's all fun and games until someone dies.

It's all fun and games until someone pukes in your car.

It's all fun and games until someone is lying in bed beside you and

You can't remember their name.

It's all fun and games until someone robs you.

It's all fun and games until someone rapes you.

It's all fun and games until...I hope you get the picture by now!

Anyone recognize this person?

ADDICTION

When you're screaming inside but you can't say a word.

You're climbing the walls but you're lying down.

Hope and faith lost their light,
The little spark just won't ignite.

The room smells like death and you don't know why.
You know there's a God; you just can't remember His name
You're spiraling, spiraling, spiraling down,
It's a very loud crash but you can't hear a sound.

I stand here screaming and wondering why.
Hurting so bad my tears ran dry.

Not knowing what to do or where to turn,
Silently watching as you crash and burn.

I FOUND JESUS

These are poems written after I truly had Jesus in my heart and was faithfully attending Ark Bible Chapel in Woodchoppertown. They have taught me so much and I think it is because everything is based on the bible. They study it and live it. Welcome was written specifically for Ark Bible Chapel, a place that always felt like home. They welcomed me when I hated myself. I hope your church feels like this. If it doesn't you might need a new church.

Ark Bible Chapel

WELCOME

Walk right in, just sit right down,

Reach for God before you drown.

It's rough out there, it's really tough.

Let Jesus fill you with all the right stuff.

Salvation and Love is waiting for you.

And there's really not much you have to do.

Love one another, Embrace your brother.

And have no Gods before your God.

Just be careful the path you trod.

Ask Jesus Christ in your heart,

He's the one to give a brand new start.

Yes, all are welcome in the House of Love,

A brand new start, a gift from above.

Search your heart.

Hey check it out.

If it's not quite right make it so,

Sit in that pew and don't let it go.

It's here for all, it's a joyous ride.

Jesus asks only that we be His bride.

My little country church, Ark Bible Chapel never gave up on me. They knew that their God is an awesome God. They knew He could do it but I think they were still amazed. This poem is fashioned after the Titanic as the ship was sinking and the band played on. Now THAT is dedication to the cause

AND THE CHURCH PRAYED ON

All other ground is sinking sand,

When's the time when you give up hope?
Say, "I won't pray anymore."
Where's the point when the battles lost, and you close the door?
Jesus said to carry on, He said to persevere.
He never said it would be easy, you may need to shed a tear.
And the Church Prayed On

Sometimes you get hurt when you out stretch your hand.
They don't seem to be listening, and it seems like sinking sand.
And the Church Prayed On

But who are we to say, how quickly they should hear,
We need to keep on trying for Christ is always near.

(Continued)

AND THE CHURCH PRAYED ON

They may need to stumble, they might even fall.

And you might be wondering are they getting this at all?

And the Church Prayed On

And then you see a step, a glimmer to give hope.

They begin to slowly change; they get off of the dope.

And quietly they start walking, in the presence of the Lord.

And you know they heard you, your faith has been restored.

And the Church Prayed On

You have been a beacon, a shelter in the storm,

A place to find God's comfort, a place to keep them warm.

All the time still praying though they didn't seem to hear,

All the time still praying, Feeling Jesus near!

For all of you out there that knows someone who's lost,

You just might be wondering is it really worth the cost?

Truly I can tell you PRAY WITH ALL YOUR HEART!

You never know where the miracle lies,

You play an important part.

The Mission Statement reflects my mantra. This is the new me.

I am the one that is striving everyday to press on toward the mark.

Philippians 3:14 KJV *I press toward the mark for the prize of the high calling of God in Christ Jesus.*

MISSION STATEMENT

I know a place of unimaginable love,

A quiet place filled with mercy and love.

A place I never knew was right here in this land.

I'm resting in my father's arms, on the solid rock I stand.

The Ark showed me a new way to live through Jesus Christ.

They taught me of forgiveness and that I must forgive,

It's unconditional love that they have to give.

Even when I fell, His love lifted me. (Even me)

They taught me to lift my head, that I could stand proud,

Because Jesus loved me as much as any other man,

The angels rejoiced on the day I asked Him into my heart.

Thought about His love and started opening my eyes to the

blessings from above.

Jesus watches over me and I try to walk in His ways,

I try to listen to the Word and let it guide me on my way.

I want to spread His Word to all who just aren't sure,

I'd like to gently guide them through the open door.

So many people are forgotten or lost.

I want to shout it out…For everyone one of us.

THE SMALL ROOM

It's a small room, but the power is strong.

This was written during a membership class at the Ark. The other couple left because they couldn't accept that Mennonites do not believe in War. They are peaceful. I stayed. Not enough drama I suppose. It was an incredibly small room but we had lots of problems and were new with Christ and prayed with passion. Pray without ceasing. Ask and you shall receive.

THE SMALL ROOM

It's a small room,

But the power is strong.

Sometimes so intense I want to break out in song.

We lay our burdens at the foot of the cross.

We see only victory, never a loss.

We pray for strength, it seems a direct line

To Gods mighty power, to the Father Divine.

You answer our prayers.

For through Jesus we pray.

No matter what the obstacle,

You make us a way.

Thank you Jesus, we know that you hear.

(Continued)

THE SMALL ROOM

You wrap your arms around us,

And show us you're near.

What a great comfort,

We need not go it alone

You walk us through the storm,

And bring us safely home.

Power and Glory,

Praise to the King,

Here it goes again

I just want to sing!

ZEAL (The Hayride)

Simple people, simple things, strong in faith to carry on.

We had just come back from a hayride. Probably the first hayride I had been on since I was very young. Actually I don't remember one when I was young. I thought how great this is: simple people, simple things, strong in faith to carry on. Dave preached on Zeal and after the sermon, it occurred to me I had some.

ZEAL

Can you see the change in me?

Can you feel the fire?

I found a brand new freedom, a love that takes me higher,

Than anything I've ever known, or thought I knew before.

I've climbed up from the Gates of Hell and

GOD was at the door.

I can't explain the energy; I only know it's real.

If I could describe it to you I guess I'd call it zeal.

Take me on a hayride I want to go and play.

Can you feel the life in me? I have so much to say.

I want to pass this on to everyone in need.

I want to light the fire; plant a brand new seed.

GOD'S love is just plain wonderful. I want the world to see,

They don't need to live in darkness, for JESUS will set them free!

Even though you find Jesus, life is not always what you are expecting. Life on life's terms is tough; we need to remember it is God molding us. **James 1:2-4 NIV** *Consider it pure joy, my brothers, whenever you face trials of many kinds, because you know that the testing of your faith develops perseverance. Perseverance must finish its work so that you may be mature and complete, not lacking anything.*

LOST

Lost, I'm here again.

Confused, I'm hurt, I'm turning to You.

Scared, I can't see the way, I know You'll lead me through.

And yet it's dark, and I often question.

It seems I can't let go, I turn my heart to You.

I'm tired, it's hard!

I can't fight any more, I know Your Love is true.

I can't see the forest for the trees,

Best I can do is drop to my knees.

I cry out, I know you hear.

Often your comfort can quiet my fears.

Thank you Jesus!

ANGST

The light on the hill must truly shine,

Not once in a while but all the time.

I didn't realize churches had politics and people had agendas. After being at the Ark for about three years we had a controversy over the youth group and the gossip started flying. I realized that these people were human and not always so nice. Through it all, I tried to stay out of it and find Jesus in this mess. Some families have since left, which I can't even imagine, and through it all we persevere. Hopefully we will become a brighter church and we will have learned something through this. Summer 2004   November 2006- We have learned a little but have far to go. 2008-I still remain and love my church.

ANGST

Out of the ashes and into the light,
Everyday a constant fight!

I kick and scratch and try so hard,
Yet deep inside my heart is scarred.

You fuss and fight and stand apart.
The people who stood by me right from the start.

None in particular, not one outstanding name,
But together you were standing, guiding me just the same.
Please come together in Jesus' name.
It's not dress rehearsal, it's not a game.

(Continued)

ANGST

The light on the hill must truly shine.

Not once in a while but all the time.

They might walk out 'cause it don't seem right.

They might not see the miracle in sight.

They might get lost, stumble or crawl,

Because the light on the hill was dark through it all.

I felt people were looking at all that is wrong and not what is right. When I first got clean I shared that my cup was not half full or empty, it was downright dry. Every day I try to see my cup half full. If I look to Jesus and develop an attitude of gratitude I will see that He has filled up my cup. He let it overflow!!!

Problem is, it is so much easier to focus on what is wrong. We had heard a sermon that day on what an encourager Paul is. It was preaching from Acts (thank you Karl). I walked out of the church determined to be the encourager. How's your cup? What have you grumbled about lately? Hey, Manna is just fine with me. I would like to reach the Promised Land.

Acts 20:1 NIV *When the uproar had ended, Paul sent for the disciples and, after encouraging them said, good-by and set out for Macedonia. He traveled through that area, speaking many words of encouragement to the people, and finally arrived in Greece, where he stayed three months.*

Ephesians 4:29-32 NIV *Do not let any unwholesome talk come out of your mouths, but only what is helpful for building others up according to their needs, that it may benefit those who listen. Verse 30: And do not grieve the Holy Spirit of God, with whom you were sealed for the day of redemption. Verse 31: Get rid of all bitterness, rage and anger, brawling, and slander, along with every form of malice. Verse 32: Be kind and compassionate to one another, forgiving each other, just as in Christ God forgave you. Smile and Encourage Someone.*

People left the church and said, "It wasn't moving."

AGAIN, ANOTHER CONFLICT AT THE CHURCH

What is moving anyway?

They say the church isn't moving.

They say the church is dead.

I'm not sure they are seeing what I see in my head.

I've seen a few get saved.

I've seen a baptism or two.

I don't think where God moves is really up to me or you.

A part of the solution is what we are called to.

And if that is not you are,

Then I ask, WHERE ARE YOU?

Encouragers-Do we follow Paul?

He is a fine example to me,

But Jesus is the one I try the most to be.

Moving, Moving, Moving forward

On any given day.

For Jesus is the truth and the light,

He is the only way.

Each year at Easter we have sunrise service at 7:00 am on top of a mountain and it's always cold. We bring blankets and shiver but I wouldn't miss it for the world. It's truly indescribable. This was written for the Easter service 2005. Imagine a mother and child bantering while you read this.

WHY ARE WE HERE?

Its cold, I'm tired I wanted to stay home.

WHY ARE WE HERE?

Mom called my name and yanked me out of bed.

WHY ARE WE HERE?

"Something about Jesus and a cross", she said.

WHY ARE WE HERE?

Why do Christians come out once a year?

Why does this date on their calendar so prominently appear?

WHY ARE WE HERE?

For every sin you've ever committed,

You may be forgiven. It's only a matter of asking.

(Continued)

WHY ARE WE HERE?

THAT'S WHY WE ARE HERE

Jesus died on the torturous cross and rose again so we may have communion with our heavenly father.

THAT'S WHY WE ARE HERE

He carried the burdens of the sins of this world and showed us amazing love.

THAT'S WHY WE ARE HERE

Words cannot express what the forgiveness and Unconditional love have meant in my life.

THAT'S WHY I AM HERE

If you want to learn about this unconditional love of Jesus, Come to the Ark next Sunday and

WE'LL GLADLY BE HERE.

John 3:16-18 NIV *For God so loved the world that HE gave His only begotten Son so whosoever believed in Him would not perish but have everlasting life. For God did not send His Son to condemn the world but to save the world through Him.*

Sorry is just an empty word unless you are sincere and make an effort to change.

SORRY

Honey I'm sorry,

I didn't mean to make you cry.

Honey don't be angry,

Don't you know I try.

Oh, I've heard the words,

The promises and more.

Don't you know I worry,

When you walk out the door?

Shattered is how I feel right now,

Not knowing where to go.

And I don't think I could take another round,

For it's familiar low.

Walk the walk.

Don't talk the talk.

Be my safe spot, my comfort,

A place that I call home.

HOW LONG?

How long do I sit here, I feel so alone?

How long should I sit here, worshiping with song?

How Long?

I wish you'd turn around and look to God.

I sit in the pew and watch families smile.

Long for you to just walk in,

And waiting all the while.

How Long?

LET'S GO TO AFRICA
(Nairobi Kenya)

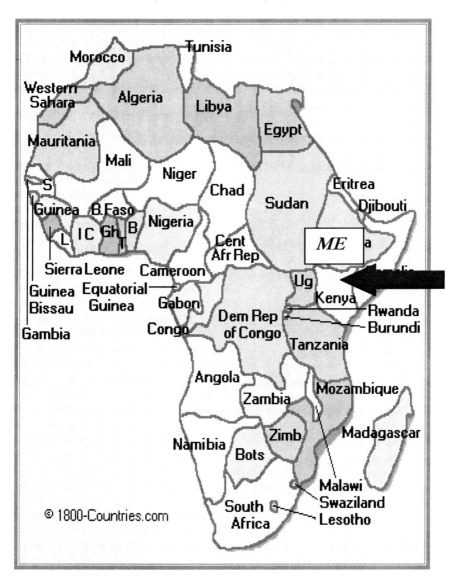

© 1800-Countries.com

- - - *111* - - -

So...When the zeal that you felt when you first were saved is fading and you know that God is still there, you've opened up your heart and your feelings are intense. So, you might ask yourself, "How do I get that zeal back?" It would appear the fire and gratitude you first felt is no longer as intense. Amazing Grace proclaims, "How precious did that grace appear the hour I first believed." Helping others is always good and you can't go wrong by helping out. I became rather involved at our church and took on many tasks such as the poetry and altar calls, as well as fruit baskets and cards to the needy. It was fulfilling, but I wanted more. The radio station I listened to was going on a trip to Africa to work in an orphanage. I so wanted to go. I signed up and worked very hard to earn four thousand and five hundred dollars ($4,500). This was my first mission experience. I thought you had to have a seminary education to be a missionary. I soon learned all you need is a desire to serve.

Once over in Kenya I realized the reason the trip was so expensive was because we were doing many tourist related things. We went out to eat often. We went to the animal orphanage and Giraffe reserve and then went on safari on the Massa Mara. I felt really bad about that. We did an outreach in a slum where people weren't able to provide food for themselves, and then we went out to eat that night. We also went to an incredibly expensive restaurant and a show. I cried that evening and walked away from the group. I was in trouble with the trip staff and they did not seem to understand my point of view. The administrator stated that they had to make the trip very attractive so people would sign up. I disagree. I listen to God's prompting and go for it. I think this is why the book is getting finalized in 2008. When I got home, I realized I would have a hard time sharing my experience, strength and hope about God's glory in Africa. I felt the funds that I had basically begged for, were misused or could've been better allocated. I spoke with someone regarding the trip and she pointed out that I had much to be grateful for and share.

When we were in the slums, there was a woman who was quite drunk. She asked why we were there. The translator said we were sharing the gospel and were doing an outreach. The girl said she wanted to know Jesus. We prayed the sinner's prayer with her.

After that point, most people started walking away. She started sobbing. I asked why she was crying and the translator said she was crying because she wanted to walk with us but didn't feel worthy. I begged the translator to tell her my story and she did. The girl held on to me with much strength hugging and kissing me. She walked with me through the slums. The funny part is that the sewers run through the slums and while we walked she was so tipsy I was sure we were going to fall to the ground and land in the sewage. Praise God we stayed upright, I had a white dress on that day.

SAVED BY GRACE!

Another wonderful thing we did was to work on an orphanage. We completed the foundation for the second story and painted, sanded, and moved dirt with very crude tools. The children of the orphanage, who were also infected with HIV, were so glad to see us. They sang of how their hope was in Jesus. They were a very shining example of how to be glad in all situations. They lost their parents, they were dying and they were playing, singing and praising God.

Again I ask...I ask you personally, is your cup half full, half empty or overflowing? It is all a matter of what you are focusing on. If you look for the blessings you will realize that they are there. Are your eyes wide open?

Africa was a very large step on my part. It was particularly unnerving because everyone on the trip listened to the radio station but went to different churches. After the twenty hour flight and mass confusion at the airport, I was feeling rather lost. I didn't know anyone and wondered what I would do if anything went wrong. I was panicking that I hadn't packed my medication. When I got to my room, I opened my suitcase and it was there. We arrived Saturday evening and I wrote Use Me on Sunday morning. Even though I was scared, I wanted God to find a way to use me. I wanted to be a part of the team and do something for someone somewhere. I was afraid to be in a different country and really afraid because I didn't know anyone. Enjoy, *Use Me.*

USE ME

Speak to me and calm my fears in this strange land.

Lord, draw me near to you so that your glory flows around me,

That your love shines through me.

USE ME

First time out it's a scary thing,

Scoop me up tuck me under your wing.

USE ME

You've changed my life, I see what you can do,

They want to see Jesus I want to see you.

USE ME

Thank You Jesus that I'm one of the flock.

You sought me out when I was quite lost

Let me give You the Glory, the Honor, the Praise!

Let me live for you in the coming days

Humble my spirit Quiet the storm

Let those around me know I live for you

We arrived on a Saturday. Life in the Lost and Found was written Sunday night after a great sermon on Mark 4:35.

That day when evening came, he said to his disciples, "Let us go over to the other side." Leaving the crowd behind, they took him along, just as he was, in the boat. There were also other boats with him. A furious squall came up, and the waves broke over the boat, so that it was nearly swamped. Jesus was in the stern, sleeping on a cushion. The disciples woke Him and said to him, "Teacher, don't you care if we drown?"

He got up, rebuked the wind and said to the waves, "Quiet! Be Still!" Then the wind died down and it was completely calm. He said to his disciples, "Why are you so afraid? Do you still have no faith?"
Isn't it funny how we panic and cry out when He is keeping us safe all along?

The church we attended that Sunday sang "What a friend we have in Jesus," a song we frequently sing at the Ark. After church I felt so welcome, I felt the prayers from home. I felt comfortable, safe, and filled with the spirit. What a difference a few hours and the scriptures can make. Enjoy Life in the Lost and Found.

LIFE IN THE LOST AND FOUND

Lost in Life, you found me.

I stood on solid rock.

I learned, I changed,

Lost in Life you found me.

I stood on solid rock

I learned, I changed, and you helped me grow.

I was lost you found me.

Chapter Two, I m here in sweet Kenya.

I was really scared,

I thought you forgot I had gone.

YOU FOUND ME!!!

The group prayed.

The sermon was peace.

It humbled me, dropped me to my knees.

I FOUND YOU

(Continued)

LIFE IN THE LOST AND FOUND

You were there all along,

Protecting me, I could not see.

You said You wouldn't leave, and of course you are true.

I was caught up and forgot what to do.

I lift my eyes up to the hills.

Where does my help come from?

My help comes from the Lord,

Maker of Heaven and Earth.

I turned, I looked, and you were there.

I FOUND YOU

"Tuesday...A Poem for Crystal," was written on the second day we were there. We were at a school outside of Runda. The people of Runda had come to join us for an outreach. I went inside a building, which resembled a plane hanger and was greeted by at least fifty (50) women who only spoke Kiswahili. I was with two other women and we were a bit overwhelmed. We had been asked to start the outreach but our translator had not arrived yet. I began singing simple songs, praying they knew the tunes. I sang, There is Power in the Blood, Jesus Loves the Little Children, and He's Got the Whole World in His Hands. They had very big smiles on their faces. They might have been laughing at me. I don't know. I am sure they were amused at what was really my best effort.

Purity, a woman from Nairobi came in to translate for us. She made it so much easier. We showed them pictures of our families and surroundings. We were just asked not to show material possessions. The women were fascinated. I wound up handing out all of the pictures I had brought along. These women fight to feed their families every day. A photograph is truly amazing to them. I also showed them pictures of snow. They were in awe. It was an overwhelming situation but I heard later that many people prayed and accepted the Lord in the other groups. PRAISE HIM! PRAISE HIM! Even in the hardest of circumstance He is with us.

Deuteronomy 31:6 NIV *Be strong and courageous. Do not be afraid or terrified because of them, for the LORD your God goes with you; he will never leave you nor forsake you. I know where my strength came from that day. Enjoy "Tuesday...A Poem for Crystal." It is named such because this occurred on Tuesday and a team member, named Crystal, really liked this poem. She cried as I read it.*

TUESDAY...A POEM FOR CRYSTAL

The children were many, we were few.

Overwhelmed, not sure what to do,

And through it all I believe Jesus shone through.

They knew no English.

We preached the Word.

In my heart I believe the gospel was heard!

I saw their homes.

It broke my heart.

Oh how I wanted to give them a brand new start!

If I could do more, I surely would.

Education, homes, jobs, and clothes,

Oh Dear Lord, if only I could.

I gave them all the love I had in my heart,

A bundle of crayons and a few sweet tarts.

They ate as if they hadn't in a while,

And all I could do was stand there and smile.

They knew no English, we preached the Word,

And I believe the gospel was heard.

As we went onto different things, the slums of Runda remained on my mind and I wrote the following poem, "Still On My Mind." These people are so down trodden and needy. Their children go to school and pass out because they have not eaten. Pray for Runda. I plan to go back and shine a little more light on Runda.

STILL ON MY MIND

They seem forgotten, yet I know you're there,
Trapped in a world that seems unfair.

End times? Maybe, but it's so bad.
I want to rejoice, but I just feel sad.

I know you watch over them with a purpose in mind.
But their life seems cruel, even unkind.

Is it because they do not seek you?
Or do they simply not know what to do?

Lord I ask mercy on this fallen land.
Build a foundation on rock not sinking sand.

We spoke the Word, I thought they heard.
Break the chains, let them gain.
Lord let them give glory to you. Let them sing praises to you.

I doubt you can imagine living in those conditions. It blows your mind. If you feel like complaining right now, just HUSH. They had few clothes, no shoes, and the sewer ran down between the huts. They had no fresh water, no electric, and very little food. Still they smiled as they saw us. A drunken woman accepted Jesus and cried because she wanted to walk with us but didn't feel worthy. I told the translator that I had been there and to tell her she was more than worthy to walk with us. She held on to me the rest of the time. This was probably the high point of my trip. Whatever is bothering you probably shouldn't be tearing you up that badly. How important is it?

When I came back I was really in culture shock. I had such a deep gratitude for life and also a disdain for those who couldn't see it

This was written today (another Tuesday) first week home. I was driving to work listening to the radio station that sponsored the trip. Dave and Emily, two DJ's from the station who accompanied us, played "The Face of Love" on the station and spoke of the trip. The Face of Love was a song we associated so deeply with those children and our trip. Why this poem came to me while driving is beyond me because I had to pull over to write it down and then I was late for work. Priorities, priorities, priorities.

WHO ARE YOU?

They are so much like us and yet worlds away,

Lost without Jesus trying to find their way.

Hawking their wares in the markets,

Telling lies while surviving the heat.

Reminds me of a car salesman,

Except they are just trying to eat.

AIDS kills people every day,

Yet the children are happy and just want to play.

Kick the can not a big rocket ship,

What a perspective, what a trip!

Side note: Do they know what rockets are?

Look inside, see who you are.

Look at them, do they seem far?

What's the priority do you need things?

Is Jesus the answer, do you desire wings?

On the radio station website several people wrote blogs to their churches. The blogs had the most joyous stories on them and spoke of many blessings. When I first came back, I felt the trip really didn't do much to glorify God .I felt there was too much tourist oriented stuff on the trip. But as I read the website I saw a different view. I realized that several people had come to the Lord and others had seen the unconditional love.

The small children who were infected with AIDS, and had lost both parents, inspired us. They were glad to see that somcone cared and they were singing songs to praise Jesus. They said their hope was in Him. I saw several things that could've been better, but through it I learned to be more careful when I select a mission trip. I also learned that God moves no matter what the circumstance. You have to look with eyes wide open so you don't miss the blessing.

A DIFFERENT VIEW

Em said, "AIDS has the face of a loving small child."

I read that line and really smiled.

Changed perceptions one more time.

Struggling to find a word that rhymes.

(Not really I just thought it was funny)

Worlds away and I am new,

Saw the joy that carries them through.

Hakuna Matata thought for the day.

Peace in the storm, God has chosen you.

Sing to the Lord a new song.

This is my story, this is my song.

Praising My Savior All the Day Long!

Blessed to have known you, Blessed to have gone,

Comparatively looking, nothing is wrong.

I was planning a trip to Nairobi, Kenya for April 19th through May 7, 2007. I was having a hard time getting people on board. I knew that even if I did not get people on board, I had learned what I wanted. I wanted to make my mission trip pleasing to the Lord, humble not flashy. I also desired to make the most of my time and financial resources while being open to what God had to show me. I wanted to follow the path that God had for me.

This section was written in 2008 as I have completed the trip and am focusing on this book. I haven't truly compiled this section but I want to give you a sense of the experience. Incredible, just bloody amazing. These would be the words I would use to describe this trip.

I went with a humble heart and wanted to maximize the money I had. Rispah, a guide I met in 2007, offered to let me stay in her home. I had no idea where she lived. When I got there, I found out she lived in a fifth floor flat directly across from Kibera slums. If you search the web you will see that Kibera is one of the largest slums in Africa. These are the hard core poor and we faithfully locked our door and did not leave the flat after dark.

I had plans of going back to Runda to help the school, as well as the orphanage, we attended the previous year and help build an additional one on their property. When I got there and began making plans, the orphanage and school were not real receptive. As I visited the orphanage, I saw that it was no further along than when we left. Politics and corruption is prevalent over there and I feel that it must have played a part the previous year.

I frequently say Plan B when my first intentions do not work out. So there I was on to Plan B. We created a day care area at Bridges Orphanage and Living Positive in Kenya. The children have no toys, therefore one of my greatest joys was to buy them lots of toys. I also purchased mattresses for both areas. One of their staple foods is Ugali. It is made from corn flour, so I provided each mother at the Living Positive Center corn flour and a blanket for their home. What a great feeling to know it was appreciated.

In the interest of humility, I must say we had no running water in our flat and we ate at home every night. I contributed money to fix the toilet to flush as I feared it might be a long three weeks. Ugali was prepared every evening and I think it tastes like concrete so I bought rice. My meals consisted of a small amount of mystery meat in juice over rice and greens. The highlight of meals was mangos and sweet bananas. We also ate chips in town. We came to call them cheap chips as you can have a bag of chips (French Fries) and a Fanta soda for less than a dollar. Our administrator advised me not to eat cheap chips with Rispah as they have no health standards really for restaurants. I could not resist as they were a great afternoon snack.

THE LIVING POSITIVE OF KENYA

The greatest joy of my trip was playing with the children in the courtyard between the buildings consisting of flats. I had chalk, bubbles, stickers, and paper with crayons in my possession. The children were on holiday (spring break) from school. Their parents aren't usually available during the day, because they have chores, work or have to look for work. The children all come to the courtyard and play. The problem is, they fight more than they play. I explained that if they wanted to play with me, they had to get along with one another. After a few days I was saying, "We play nice because we are friends," every time they argued. After a week, the other children were saying it when someone acted up. It was well understood that if you wanted Ms. Sheila to come out, you had to play nice. Eventually the children from the slums came over to join in. Before I left, the children drew me pictures and I probably have twenty plus drawings that say, "We play nice because we are friends."

This was a most unexpected area of service but I think it glorified God more than I could've hoped to do. Lines 1 through 4 of the following poem are the little rap song we sang to one another.

What love, what a blessing, God bless the children. Enjoy Playing Nice .

WE PLAY NICE BECAUSE WE ARE FRIENDS!

PLAYING NICE

We play nice because we're friends.

We will share to the very end.

We don't push we don't shove,

Cause down on the block it's all about love.

Yes I fell in love with them,

And every day we played.

I taught them please and thank you,

They seemed like foreign words.

I taught them life is better,

If we follow the written Word.

God is so amazing!

He shows up where you are.

He points you to the mission, however near or far.

My God is a God of so much more.

His acts are more than I thought I'd see.

Ideas I couldn't think of,

Cause He is wiser than me.

PLAYING NICE!

Pray for Kenya. Pray for My Children.
Pray for World Peace.

This concludes the 2007 trip. There was much more but I don't want to write a novel. The area is currently in political unrest and actually unsafe to travel to. The slums I walked through are actually burned out in sections and many people were displaced or killed. Pray for Kenya. Pray for my children. Pray for World Peace.

I will return but I will value my safety right now. Don't get me wrong, I cry for them, pray for them and will help as God leads me. Still on my mind is probably so much more appropriate for the children of the third district and Kibera. They are the innocents caught in the crossfire.

I HEAR JESUS CALLING

THINGS I HAVE LEARNED

1. Christian Music

When I first got saved I was told when Jesus came back the trumpet would sound. I had just found Contemporary Christian music and had it rather loud. I turned down the radio and called the woman who helped me get saved. I was very concerned that if I had the radio up too loud I would miss it when the trumpet sounds. She reassured me I would hear it. I felt better and cranked it back up.

The lesson is:
Should Jesus come back you will know.

2. Gods Grace

When at Ida's home for that first bible study the others were speaking of Mosaic Law. They said, "We are no longer under it." I was thinking it was a mosaic tile art piece or something artsy. I later asked and was told that it meant that since Jesus came we no longer needed to follow all the rules of the days of Moses. We only have to love one another, do everything out of love, and have no other Gods before our God.

The lesson is:
Mosaics are beautiful tile art but they aren't laws.

3. Grace and Mercy

This was written by Paul:

(Continued)

THINGS I HAVE LEARNED

1 Timothy 1:12-14 NIV

I thank Christ Jesus our Lord, who has given me strength, that he considered me faithful, appointing me to his service. Even though I was once a blasphemer, a persecutor, and a violent man, I was shown mercy because I acted in ignorance and unbelief. The grace of our Lord was poured out on me abundantly, along with the faith and love that are in Christ Jesus.

Ephesians 2:8-10 NIV

For it is by grace you have been saved, through faith—and this not from yourselves, it is the gift of God—not by works, so that no one can boast. For we are God's workmanship, created in Christ Jesus to do good works, which God prepared in advance for us to do.

The lesson is:

Grace is something that you receive that you don't deserve. Mercy is that we don't receive what we deserve.

4. Judgment

Matthew 7:1-6 NIV

"Do not judge, or you too will be judged. For in the same way you judge others, you will be judged, and with the measure you use, it will be measured to you. "Why do you look at the speck of sawdust in your brother's eye and pay no attention to the plank in your own eye? How can you say to your brother, 'Let me take the speck out of your eye,' when all the time there is a plank in your own eye? You hypocrite, first take the plank out of your own eye, and then you will see clearly to remove the speck from your brother's eye."

(Continued)

THINGS I HAVE LEARNED

People who judge don't matter; People who matter don't judge.

The lesson is:

Until God comes down and asks for my help in judging someone, I think I will leave that to Him.

5. Life doesn't get easier, we learn to cope.

In every situation we are given a choice. We can wallow in what is wrong or ask God for strength to walk on. Life happens and we can't change that. All we can do is look for solutions.

The lesson is:

Suicide is a very permanent solution to a temporary problem.

6. Gratitude

Psalm 118:24 NIV

This is the day the LORD has made; let us rejoice and be glad in it.

Attitude is the key here. How do you see your life? Is your cup half full, half empty, dry or overflowing? When I first got clean, I would share at NA meetings that my cup was dry because it was cracked. As time progressed, that attitude changed even though the circumstances didn't. This takes some practice. Something to help you in this process is to praise Him in the storm. Most animals hide when a storm is coming. Buffalo face it head on and run through it to get to the other side. Be a buffalo. Develop an attitude of

(Continued)

gratitude. There is always someone worse off than you. Recovery says, "This too shall pass." This is usually true. Make a list of all the blessings you have received or all the prayer requests that came true. This should help and your cup should appear to overflow. God has a purpose for these trials.

The lesson is:
Every day is a holiday, every meal a feast.

7. Dreamers

All of us do time in the darkness, dreamers learn to steer by the stars. All of us do time in the gutter, dreamers learn to look at the cars. There is blood running in the streets don't let it be yours. TURN AROUND and walk the razors edge. Keep moving. TURN AROUND. This is taken from a RUSH song I truly enjoy. Sometimes we are standing on the razors edge and we need to look at the stars rather than focus on the darkness. If we have faith it will soon be the dawn of a new day.

The lesson is:
If you are daring enough to think it, then do it, achieve it, Dream BIG.

8. Live well, laugh often.

Bill Cosby
"Through humor, you can soften some of the worst blows that life delivers. And once you find laughter, no matter how painful your situation might be, you can survive it."

(Continued)

THINGS I HAVE LEARNED

1 Thessalonians 5:16-18 NIV

Be joyful always; pray continually; give thanks in all circumstances, for this is God's will for you in Christ Jesus.

James 1:2-6 NIV

Consider it pure joy, my brothers, whenever you face trials of many kinds, because you know that the testing of your faith develops perseverance. Perseverance must finish its work so that you may be mature and complete, not lacking anything. If any of you lacks wisdom, he should ask God, who gives generously to all without finding fault, and it will be given to him. But when he asks, he must believe and not doubt, because he who doubts is like a wave of the sea, blown and tossed by the wind.

2 Corinthians 6:4-10 NIV

Rather, as servants of God we commend ourselves in every way: in great endurance; in troubles, hardships and distresses; in beating, imprisonments and riots; in hard work, sleepless nights and hunger, in purity, understanding, patience and kindness; in the Holy Spirit and in sincere love; in truthful speech and in the power of God; with weapons of righteousness in the right hand and in the left, through glory and dishonor, bad report and good report; genuine, yet regarded as impostors, known, yet regarded as unknown; dying and yet we live on beaten, and yet not killed; sorrowful, yet always rejoicing, poor, yet making many rich; having nothing and yet possessing everything.

The lesson is:
Energy is Contagious Laughter is Infectious.

9. Be a New Person.   (Continued)

THINGS I HAVE LEARNED

Ephesians 4:22-24 NIV

You were taught, with regard to your former way of life, to put off your old self, which is being corrupted by its deceitful desires; to be made new in the attitude of your minds; and to put on the new self, created to be like God in true righteousness and holiness.

2 Corinthians 5:17-19 NIV

Therefore, if anyone is in Christ, he is a new creation; the old has gone, the new has come! All this is from God, who reconciled us to himself through Christ and gave us the ministry of reconciliation: that God was reconciling the world to himself in Christ, not counting men's sins against them. And he has committed to us the message of reconciliation. There is always someone in a worse situation than you.

The lesson is:
The Lord transforms people into an image that is more beautiful than anything we can hope to imagine.

10. BE HAPPY…He'll make a way

1 Corinthians 10:13 NIV

No temptation has seized you except what is common to man. And God is faithful; He will not let you be tempted beyond what you can bear. But when you are tempted, He will also provide a way out so that you can stand up under it.

The lesson is:
If we DO NOT keep a good attitude and have faith in the Lord there will be: no joy in Mudville.

(Continued)

THINGS I HAVE LEARNED

11. People will disappoint you but God will never fail you.

2 Thessalonians 3:3 NIV

But the Lord is faithful, and he will strengthen and protect you from the evil one.

The lesson is:
People are like chapters in our life story. Turn the page.

12. Show me don't tell me.

If you talk the talk, walk the walk. Many people sound good in public but run wild when out of sight. Stick with the winners, the ones whose life you admire. Do you want what they have? Do they live what they preach? This is one of the most important tools for growth. Don't be like the hypocrites and Pharisees.

Mathew 23:25 NIV

Woe to you, teachers of the law and Pharisees, you hypocrites! You clean the outside of the cup and dish, but inside they are full of greed and self-indulgence.

3 John 1:3-4 NIV

It gave me great joy to have some brothers come and tell about your faithfulness to the truth and how you continue to walk in the truth. I have no greater joy than to hear that my children are walking in the truth.

The lesson is:
Be consistent, be pure. You cannot tell a can by its label or a book by its cover. (Except mine) (Continued)

THINGS I HAVE LEARNED

13. Beauty

I have seen many beautiful things in my life and I believe that God puts them there to remind us that He is God. Where I live the leaves change colors in the fall. Others enjoy beaches and others see snow covered mountaintops. These are very simple examples of beauty but how much more does he show us through the Swiss Alps, the Serengeti or the Grand Canyon. He put a little beauty in every part of the world so we may all experience it. It varies in each region but no one can deny it is there.

The lesson is:
When you see a beautiful sunrise or sunset remember it is hand painted by God.

14. If I could wave my magic wand I'd set everyone free.

Wow, what a thought. Unfortunately life doesn't work that way. People often don't tap into the resources available to them. They feel self-sufficient and decide they don't need a God. These are the mean people, the violent offenders and the people who die in the streets. Sometimes they are everyday people, walking around angry all the time. They might even be people in your own home or maybe even you. There are chains holding us that only God can break and that is only if we let Him.

The lesson is:
We are powerless to change someone else, remember they can only change themselves.

Fear not, THERE IS ALWAYS HOPE

Martin Luther King Jr.

If you lose hope, somehow you lose the vitality that keeps life moving, you lose that courage to be, that quality that helps you go on in spite of it all. And so today I still have a dream.

Pearl S. Buck

None who have always been free can understand the terrible fascinating power of the hope of freedom to those who are not free.

Christopher Reeve

Once you choose hope, anything's possible.

Author Unknown

When the world says, "Give up,"
Hope whispers, "Try it one more time."

George Iles

Hope is faith holding out its hand in the dark…

Charles L. Allen

When you say a situation or a person is hopeless, you're slamming the door in the face of God.

Jose' Joaquin Olmedo

He who does not hope to win has already lost.

(Continued)

Thomas Fuller

If it were not for hopes, the heart would break.

Albert Einstein

"Learn from yesterday, live for today, hope for tomorrow."

Thich Nhat Hanh

Hope is important because it can make the present moment less difficult to bear. If we believe that tomorrow will be better, we can bear a hardship today.

Romans 5:5 NIV

And hope does not disappoint us, because God has poured out his love into our hearts by the Holy Spirit, whom he has given us.

Hebrews 11:1 NIV

Now faith is being sure of what we hope for and certain of what we do not see.

So, my husband holds me in his arms and we both cry. I asked him, "How two people who love each other so much could be so far apart?" He says he doesn't know. He knows I am working on this book and he picks it up and reads the part about hope. He says, "I wonder what the next chapter looks like?" I say, "I wish I knew."

I'm moving forward not knowing where I am going. But fear not, **THERE IS ALWAYS HOPE!**

This is not a false alarm, this is not a test, this is not a dress rehearsal, this is life. Show up, suit up and go along for the ride. Move, dream, and hope. Don't be content because people who are content don't move, don't change and are stuck on the comfy sofa. Press on to the mark. Heed the call, find your gifts, seek your purpose and fulfill it for God's glory. Wake up from your slumber and just do it…

I hear Jesus calling.

Sheila

AUTHOR'S COMMENTARY BY SHEILA ANDRIEN

Hang on, Hope is available! I didn't give God much thought until I was the age of thirty-six (36). Up until that point I figured I was going to hell, so why try? If you do not know the salvation plan, the words Jesus Saves flashing over the rescue mission don't mean much. The bottom line of that plan is that we are all forgiven, all our sins have been taken away and we get another chance at life if we ask Jesus in our hearts and come to God through Jesus. That's it. It is that simple.

One thing that occurs to me, looking back, is that the unacceptable became acceptable. Things you would never dream of doing or experiencing just kind of happen. Not only do they happen, you also accept them. Today the unacceptable is no longer acceptable or tolerated. I go out of my way to keep peace while being assertive. I also avoid chaos and madness as much as possible

All the stuff we have done becomes just that, only stuff. It no longer has a hold on us through guilt and shame because we are forgiven. We can now have communion with God and look forward to Heaven on Earth and after we die. When they explained to me that I was forgiven through the blood of Jesus and had another chance, I was amazed. All these years of thinking I was condemned, only to find out I had a chance. Who knew? I am not condemned for all time and I can turn this around. It is a new day dawning. What a difference! I didn't believe them at first but when they showed me verse after verse backing this up, and blessing after blessing (that I thought was good luck) Well, how can you deny it? Again, if God pulls you from the muck and mire and completely transforms your life to the point you don't even recognize it, how could you not share it? If I can get it, you can get it and if we can find hope to carry on, it is worth it.

Printed in the United States
206758BV00002B/403-516/P

9 780976 854074